Essene Book of Meditations and Blessings

by DANAAN PARRY

Printed on recycled paper
Illustrated by Susan Hand

Typesetting/revision: Healing Pages, healingpgs@aol.com

Original cover design by Diane Addesso

ISBN: 0965380874

© 1991, 2000 Earthstewards Network Publications

Published by
Earthstewards Network Publications
PO Box 10697, Bainbridge Island WA 98110
800-561-2909

Sales of this book help support the Earthstewards Network, a nonprofit organization co-founded by Danaan Parry.

For more information, please visit www.earthstewards.org

ALL RIGHTS RESERVED

Second edition
First published September 2000

table of contents

how to use this book	5
the essenes	7
the essene's physical communions	8
meditations & blessings	11

      winter solstice
      imbolc
      spring equinox
      beltane
      summer solstice
      teltane
      autumn equinox
      samhain

essenes & me	139
about danaan parry	142
earthstewards network	143

how to use this book

This little book was adapted from the *Essene Book of Days*. Use it as a travel companion. Carry it with you through the day as a gentle reminder of the daily and seasonal focus.

Following the earth's seasonal cycle, the meditations and blessings are divided into eight seasonal sections, with a meditation and blessing for each day of the week.

The solstice or equinox marks the start of each season, which is then subdivided by the cross-quarter day falling halfway in-between.

These cross-quarter days have different names in different cultures. Danaan Parry used their Celtic names of Imbolc, Beltane, Teltane, and Samhain.

Within each of the eight seasonal sections, you will find a specific meditation and blessing to use for each day of the week during that time period as well as the seasonal and spiritual focus for that time of the year.

The daily meditations and blessings correspond to the Essene focus for that day, as described in the section on daily physical attunements.

With this second edition, we've also added new pages to help you to maintain your journal on your travels.

Further information on sun and moon signs, rituals, descriptions of holidays and more room to record your daily feelings can be found in the *Essene Book of Days*.

We hope that our books comfort and inspire you in your growth. More information on the Earthstewards Network, our publications, and Danaan Parry's legacy can be found at the end of this book.

the essenes

Discovery of the Dead Sea Scrolls in 1947, in a series of caves near the Dead Sea, brought to new light the wisdom-teachings of the Essene communities. These peaceful people lived in spiritual communities in the Middle East more than 2,000 years ago. The Essenes lived in harmony with the earth and seasonal cycles and developed physical communions for each day of the week.

Their communities were dedicated to preserving the ancient teachings and to preparing the way for the new age of Pisces, when Christ energy would flood the world.

They lived in simple harmony with all of nature, following the spiritual wisdom of their inner voices, which the Buddhists call "living one's dharma." Their spiritual practices allowed them to absorb and channel the vibrations and healing powers of the plants, the sun, and the four elements of earth, air, fire, and water, for their own nourishment and for the healing of the earth itself. We have much to learn from these simple folk.

The Essene teachings tell us that John the Baptist was an Essene master, and that he and other Essene teachers trained the initiate Jesus in the ancient wisdom during that 20-year period of his life about which the Bible is silent.

meditations & blessings

The meditations and blessings recorded on the following pages were inspired by the Essenes. These verses reflect the final revisions made by Danaan Parry for the *Essene Book of Days* prior to his death in 1996.

Daily Physical Communions

It was of the highest importance to the Essene communities that the world of the spirit would be integrated with the world of the flesh. They practiced not only a mental but also a physical communion to the higher forces.

The following daily attunements are in keeping with this Essene practice. Combined with daily meditation, they can be used to connect intimately the world of the spirit, mind, and physical body that exist within your being.

Saturday

The beginning of the Essene week is devoted to good consciousness. If possible, reserve this day for fasting. Take in only water, or perhaps some juice or herbal tea. If fasting is not possible every Saturday, consume as little food as is necessary, and become highly conscious of the quality and the benefits of the food. Attune your body to the vibration of the liquid or food, so that you become nourished by its essence. In this way, water alone can become your food of life.

Sunday

A day devoted to tending to the earth. In the spirit of regeneration, healing, and abundance, give as much time as possible to creative work in the garden. This garden may be your backyard garden, a communal farm, your rosebushes or a small section of your city park that cries out for loving care. The focus is on your role as a steward of your planet, and on learning to absorb life energy from the plants and to give it back again.

Monday

A day of silence. Change nothing in your daily routine with the exception of talking. Allow the world to deal with your silence, and be fully conscious of how you deal with it. Contemplate the many alternative ways of relating and communication, and how the medium of speech at times dilutes the intensity of our relationships. Write in your journal about your experience.

Tuesday

A day of simple contemplation of the joy of life, the fullness of your blessings. After morning meditation and breakfast, take an extended walk in a natural setting, silently. Avoid distractions, and focus on the colors, smells, and the state of nature at this point in the seasonal cycle. If a morning walk is not possible, any time of day or night will do. The focus is on creation of a silent, meditative walk through nature, becoming one with your surroundings Write in your journal afterwards.

Wednesday

Here the focus is on the sun, allowing its power and light to enter your body. Rise early and go to a place where you can observe sunrise. Begin your morning meditation as the first rays of the sun bathe your body. If possible, allow the sun's rays to nourish your naked body this day, even when the weather is cold.

Thursday

A day of purification, of cleansing all the bodies of you. Carry the spirit of purification with you into meditation. Arrange to bathe your body in a leisurely, contemplative atmosphere. Consider the connections between your own water, your blood, and the waters of life. Consider the sap in trees, the rivers, lakes, and oceans, the circulatory system of our Mother the Earth. Lengthy immersions in hot and cold tubs are of value, as is an occasional enema for internal cleansing (no more than once a month, unless recommended for healing of a particular condition).

Friday

The inbreath and outbreath of the universe is contemplated through long periods of controlled breathing. During meditation, alternately block the left and right nasal passages, taking ten breaths through each. Throughout the day, continually bring your awareness to your breath, taking long, deep inhalations frequently.

Contemplate your Stillpoint, which occurs between exhalation and inhalation. It is the point where we "die" at each outbreath and are reborn with each inbreath. Write in your journal.

winter solstice
december

spiritual focus for this season

saturday
i will bring the spirit of
giving to _____
sunday
i will bring the spirit of
calmness to _____
monday
i will bring the spirit of
honesty to _____
tuesday
i will bring the spirit of
joy to _____
wednesday
i will bring the spirit of
courage to _____
thursday
i will bring the spirit of
contentment to _____
friday
i will bring the spirit of
newness to _____

feelings:

_____

_____

_____

_____

seasonal focus:
the seed stirs in the earth.

saturday

morning focus
Our Earthly Mother

meditation
I am bathed in an ocean
Of love and guidance
As I begin my journey
Out from the center.
All the earth nourishes me
And I return this nourishment
As love.
As the wisdom of the Mother
Slowly urges me to new awareness,
I joyfully surrender
The safety of the womb
So as to experience my part
In the unfolding plan of Light.

evening focus
The angel of Eternal Life

the blessing
As the long night slowly yields to day,
Even as the old millennium
Surrenders to the new,
I, too, surrender to my next step
Which carries me toward
My natural state of limitlessness.
The winter teaches me of inner abundance,
Inner completeness,
As I now prepare for the outer learning
That this new year brings.

Winter Solstice

feelings:

_____

_____

_____

_____

seasonal focus:
the seed stirs in the earth.

sunday

morning focus
The angel of Earth

meditation
From the calm place
At my spiritual center
I have touched the wisdom
Of the earth in winter.
Regeneration streams
From the holy earth to me,
And I am full.
I now gather to me the lessons
Which will empower me
To channel this life-giving earth force
For the good of all beings.

evening focus
The angel of Creative Work

the blessing
The winter's journey
To the source of inner creativity
Now turns and guides me slowly
Toward outward manifestation.
Depth will be fulfilled in expansion
As I contemplate
My dharmic path of service.
I give thanks for the Mother's gifts
Which have brought me to this.

feelings:

_____

_____

_____

_____

seasonal focus:
the seed stirs in the earth.

monday

morning focus
The angel of Life

meditation
Slowly the balance shifts from inner creativity
To outer manifestation.
Slowly my core of inner strength
Streams outward
Along my nervous system,
Bringing health and vitality
To the whole of my being.
The life in me prepares itself,
Strengthens itself for the moment
In the cycle
When it will overflow its bounds,
Surging toward a oneness
With all of life.

evening focus
The angel of Peace

the blessing
I evoke the forces of peace and harmony
And ask these forces
To prepare me as a channel
For their overlighting guidance.
My heart swells with thanksgiving
For a winter of inner preparation
Which will lead me to the first step
In becoming a channel for peace:
That of finding peace
Within my own being.

feelings:

___

___

___

___

seasonal focus:
the seed stirs in the earth.

tuesday

morning focus
The angel of Joy

meditation

Wherein lies the source of joy?
The inner peace of winter
Prepares me for the answer;
It shouts quietly to me,
"Do not seek happiness; seek rather
Your true nature,
Your true reason for being;
Seek your dharma.
Joy is the child of completeness,
Of living your dharma."
At this time of new, small beginnings,
I feel the clarity of vision growing in me,
And I am pregnant with joy.

evening focus
The angel of Power

the blessing

The silent stirring of the new life in me
Fills me with an inner strength.
The strength is good;
And it comes from a place
Deep inside my being
That has only been reached
In the depth of ego-death.
This power I trust;
This is the power
Of love and compassion
The world cries out for.
The veil of illusion
Lifts slowly and reveals
The direction of my path.

Winter Solstice

feelings:

_____

_____

_____

_____

seasonal focus:
the seed stirs in the earth.

wednesday

morning focus
The angel of the Sun

meditation
The promise, the prophecy, is within me.
That which I have waited for is now present.
No longer need I fear.
Within me shines
The first glimmering of the Light,
And I am filled with the awareness
That the fulfilling of the prophecy
Is not a thing apart from me;
It *is* me.
As the first small rays of the sun
Return to my world,
I, too, return slowly to the world of form.
I humbly accept the mantle
Of that which I AM.
As I merge my light
With the light of all the beings of Light,
I surrender to my own divinity.

evening focus
The angel of Love

the blessing
Life, you are a profound
Expression of Love.
The gentle, quiet expansion
Of the winter-mother's love
Fills me with inner joy.
I bow before the purity of this love
Which nourishes without attachment.

feelings:

_____

_____

_____

_____

seasonal focus:
the seed stirs in the earth.

thursday

morning focus
The angel of Water

meditation
As the clear winter water
Nourishes the seed within the earth,
I am nourished by new-found awareness
Of who I truly am.
This awareness
Has not yet fully matured,
And I rest content
In the arms of the unfolding universe,
Which will reveal all wisdom
In its time.
The Power of the unmanifest
Even now works
Within my spiritual heart,
And I am at peace.

evening focus
The angel of Wisdom

the blessing
I call upon my own internal voice,
Which is ever linked
With the universal voice
Of inner knowing.
I ask, as I slowly move
From winter's inner development
To the first stirrings of outer work,
That I be given the strength
To trust my own still small voice,
Whose guidance is never faulty.
For this blessing I give thanks.

feelings:

_____

_____

_____

_____

seasonal focus:
the seed stirs in the earth.

Friday

Morning Focus
The angel of Air

Meditation
There is a force in me,
Pushing, pushing,
Beginning its outbreath
After a long sleep.
Sacred darkness slowly yields
To newborn light.
As I move outward
From the stillpoint of outer death
To share my new-found breath of life
With all,
I shall never forget
The inbreath of the Mother
That nurtured me
Through the winter's night.

Evening Focus
Our Heavenly Father

The Blessing
I ask that the Light,
The Creative Force of the universe,
Breathe the cleansing outbreath of spirit
Into my heart and my deeds.
I rejoice in this time of promise,
Of new stirrings,
Of the rebirth of the lotus
Which will one day
Open fully to God.

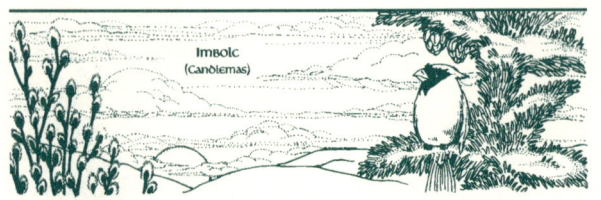

feelings:

_____

_____

_____

_____

seasonal focus:
BROOKS RUN FREE AND BUDS APPEAR.

imbolc
february 1

spiritual focus for this season

saturday
i will bring the spirit of planetary stewardship to _____

sunday
i will bring the spirit of fullness to _____

monday
i will bring the spirit of uniqueness to _____

tuesday
i will bring the spirit of growth to _____

wednesday
i will bring the spirit of connectedness to

_____

thursday
i will bring the spirit of oneness to _____

friday
i will bring the spirit of laughter to _____

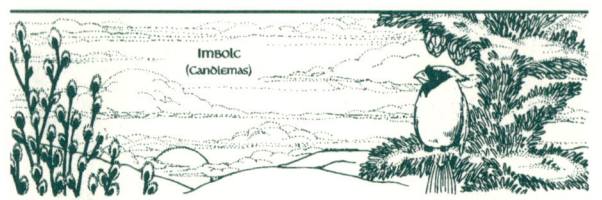

feelings:

___

___

___

___

seasonal focus:
brooks run free and buds appear.

saturday

morning focus
Our Earthly Mother

meditation
The path of the spirit calls to me to grow,
And grow I will.
But the journey home will take me
Far from my roots
Before I can once again
Return to the source.
Mother, at this time of new outer growth,
Fill my being with your love.
While my roots still are young,
Teach me to use Mind as servant,
Never as master.

evening focus
The angel of Eternal Life

the blessing
At this time of newness,
Of moving faster into the unknown,
Let me never forget that while I am
I am also old.
There is an ancient part of me
That will provide the source of knowing
As my newness wanders forth
To seek its true identity.
I am new. I am ancient.
I AM.

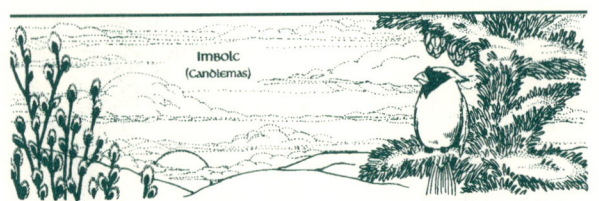

feelings:

___

___

___

___

seasonal focus:
BROOKS RUN FREE AND BUDS APPEAR.

sunday

morning focus
The angel of Earth

meditation

There is a part of me
That is rooted firmly in the earth.
It is to this grounded, solid me
That I now deeply bow.
For without this,
There could be no expansion,
No life-giving nourishment
Coursing to my tender new leaves,
No strong stem to reach
Toward the sun.
The earth is my home
For this incarnation,
And I am blessed.

evening focus
The angel of Creative Work

the blessing

There is a sacredness which infuses my life
As I realize that my own growth is my work.
I am the canvas
I am the artist
I am the paint.
I ask that the artist be ever guided
By the Artist,
And that as I grow,
I come to know
The perfection
Of the unfinished masterpiece
That is Life.

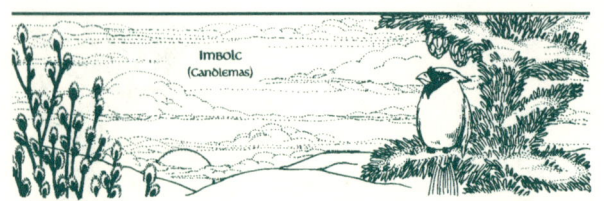

feelings:

_____

_____

_____

_____

seasonal focus:
brooks run free and buds appear.

monday

morning focus
The angel of Life

meditation
And now the life-force in me,
As in all beings,
Cries out to know itself
Apart from the Mother.
My life,
The uniqueness of that which I am,
Calls to me to experience,
For it is only in the full freedom
Of my own experiencing
That I gain the wisdom
Of my connectedness
With all that is.
For I am the one
And I am also the many.

evening focus
The angel of Peace

the blessing
As I experience the new life in me
Bursting its bounds,
I ask to be made more clearly aware
Of my part in the Plan,
That I may prepare myself
To become the fullest expression and channel
For peace.

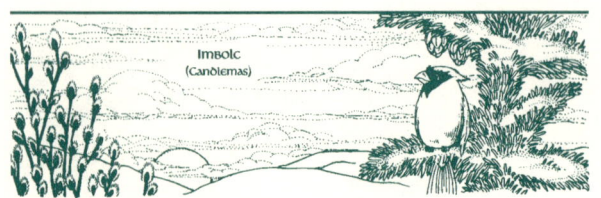

Imbolc
(Candlemas)

feelings:

_____

_____

_____

_____

seasonal focus:
brooks run free and buds appear.

tuesday

morning focus
The angel of Joy

meditation
How strong in me is my need to grow
To expand
To meet the promise of
The coming spring.
There is a joy in me
That carries me onward
From this physical being
To the awareness of the cosmic ocean
Of Love
In which I dwell.
May I be blessed
To share this joy with all beings,
In whatever way I can.

evening focus
The angel of Power

the blessing
There is a Power
At work in the world
Which assists each living thing
To rise above its prison
Of desire and attachment,
And to soar
In the freedom of God's love.
I place myself in the path of this Power
And surrender to the divine Will
That charts the course of the path.
It is this Power
That allows me to grow.

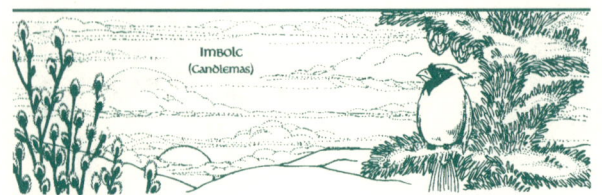
Imbolc
(Candlemas)

feelings:

_____

_____

_____

_____

seasonal focus:
BROOKS RUN FREE AND BUDS APPEAR.

wednesday

morning focus
The angel of the Sun

meditation
As the force of new life wells up in me,
I hear the far call
Of my ancient spiritual father, the sun.
This is a time for reaching upward,
A time for growing toward the sky
As I still draw nourishment
From my mother the earth.
I am the link;
I am the channel
Between the sun and the earth.
I am the life.

evening focus
The angel of Love

the blessing
Mother, you are love in me,
Overflowing,
And I bless you as I grow.
Father, you are love in me,
Guiding me,
And I bless you as I strive to know
My true nature.
Soon my buds will open,
And my own young channel
Of love
Will be available for you
To use to heal the earth.

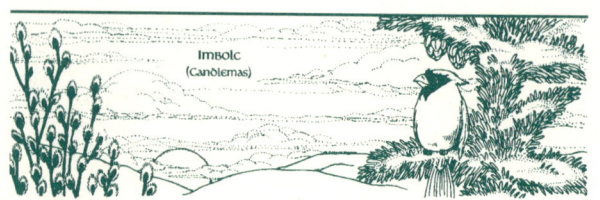

feelings:

___

___

___

___

seasonal focus:
BROOKS RUN FREE AND BUDS APPEAR.

thursday

morning focus
The angel of Water

meditation
About me flow
The waters of nourishment;
Within me flows
The water of nourishment.
My bloodstream is
Aglow with the impulse of life
As I challenge
The dark places in my being,
As I expand beyond
The security of the womb,
As I move past my own definitions.
And surrounding this, engulfing me,
Is the cosmic ocean of Love and Light
From whence I truly came.

evening focus
The angel of Wisdom

the blessing
I pause to honor
The overlighting stream of wisdom
That guides each living thing
On its journey home.
That journey is my journey;
That home is my home;
And that wisdom is as alive in me
As it is in the highest of beings.
As I grow in spiritual maturity,
I see that this wisdom is always available
To the extent that I have prepared myself
To receive it.

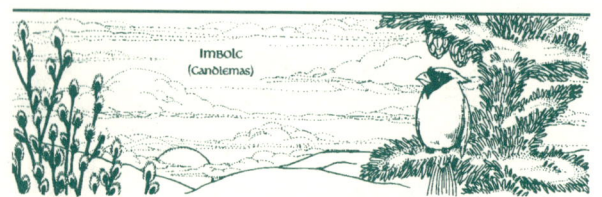

feelings:

_____

_____

_____

_____

seasonal focus:
BROOKS RUN FREE AND BUDS APPEAR.

friday

morning focus
The angel of Air

meditation
The earth, long my home
Through the dark of winter,
Has yielded to the morning breath of air.
The Plan now urges me to outbreathe,
To expand to meet my destiny.
Why am I here?
For what have I returned this time?
And the air breathes
Its laughing answer past me.
"You are life.
You are the all in the process
Of becoming One.
Experience yourself."

evening focus
Our Heavenly Father

the blessing
What is this that gently forces me
From the still safe place of inaction?
What force compels me
To abandon my comfort
Of well-worn despair?
Our Heavenly Father does not work from without,
But from within my own heart.
As the Law manifests itself through Love,
I stand in humble awe of the part of God that I AM.

feelings:

___

___

___

___

seasonal focus:
buds unfold to early flowers.

spring equinox
march

spiritual focus for this season

saturday
i will bring the spirit of
humility to _____
sunday
i will bring the spirit of
openess to _____
monday
i will bring the spirit of
freedom to _____
tuesday
i will bring the spirit of
excitement to _____
wednesday
i will bring the spirit of
completeness to _____
thursday
i will bring the spirit of
perfection to _____
friday
i will bring the spirit of
sharing to _____

feelings:

_____

_____

_____

_____

seasonal focus:
buds unfold to early flowers.

saturday

morning focus
Our Earthly Mother

meditation
Mother, in this season of the flowers
I bow to you in humble awe.
The brilliant colors of my blossoms
Are growing now,
Soon to be fruit.
I feel the need to give to you
For all that you have given to me,
And though the moment is not yet right,
One day my fruit will yield its seed
To your sweet earth.

evening focus
The angel of Eternal Life

the blessing
In the joyful outbreath
Of this season of my growth,
It is difficult to remember
The cycles of my life.
But remember I will,
For it is the rhythm of my living/dying
That gives the meaning to my journey,
And it is the surrender of yesterday's fruit
That allows the new seed to grow
To flower.

feelings:

_____

_____

_____

_____

seasonal focus:
buds unfold to early flowers.

sunday

morning focus
The angel of Earth

meditation
My petals spread upward to the sun,
My roots dig deeply in the earth.
Outward streams my love
To touch all life,
Inward streams the love
Life shares with me.
Let me open fully to it all,
For love and life and growth
Come in many colors
And sing many different songs.

evening focus
The angel of Creative Work

the blessing
The season's work comes clear to me,
Amidst my outward growth.
To love it all,
The bitter and the sweet,
For each is drawn to me,
Bringing lessons
To aid my journey home.
How blessed is the student,
How wise the teacher.
And are they not the same?

feelings:

_____

_____

_____

_____

seasonal focus:
buds unfold to early flowers.

monday

morning focus
The angel of Life

meditation
My life is guided onward
Toward the Light.
All about me are the signs of growth,
The signs of new life
Bursting from containment.
I, too, feel this primal urge
To cast off limitation
And open my petals to the sun.
No longer must I wait.
I share my life with those I love.

evening focus
The angel of Peace

the blessing
Beauty surrounds me, beauty all around me.
Quiet beauty of the new flowers of springtime
Within me, the peaceful beauty of my being
Reflects the richness of my life.
And I am blessed.

feelings:

___

___

___

___

seasonal focus:
buds unfold to early flowers.

tuesday

morning focus
The angel of Joy

meditation
I am conscious of nature's outward thrust
In this season of the flowers,
And my heart is filled with joy.
The colors of my world,
The colors of my being,
The excitement of my life,
All these are the love of God
Shining upon my spirit.
There is no more that I need,
For I am complete.

evening focus
The angel of Power

the blessing
The joyful thrust of all of life,
Reaching for the sun,
Reminds me of the power that is mine
In the service of the Light.
May I remember always
That I am the server,
And that God is the Power.

feelings:

___

___

___

___

seasonal focus:
buds unfold to early flowers.

wednesday

morning focus
The angel of the Sun

meditation
The cells within my being
Respond to the call of
My spiritual father,
The sun.
As I grow,
As I expand to fill the outer limits
Of my potential,
I am nourished by the warmth
Of our ancient star
And I have all that
I could ever need
To guide me safely home.

evening focus
The angel of Love

the blessing
Who could not see,
Who could not feel,
The expression of divine Love
That fills the world this day?
As my buds softly open
Into rainbow flowers,
I return this Love
In every way I can.

feelings:

_____

_____

_____

_____

seasonal focus:
buds unfold to early flowers.

thursday

morning focus
The angel of Water

meditation
In my upward movement
Toward the perfect flower
That I truly am,
What feeds my inner being
But the waters of the earth,
Given by the Father to the Mother
And given back again?
Waters of the Spirit,
Waters of the earth,
Fill me fully with your life
And make me whole.

evening focus
The angel of Wisdom

the blessing
There is a knowing in this universe
That opens flowers in their time,
That gives me strength to grow.
The wisdom of this primal source
Is always mine to tap,
For I am one with all,
And all is mine to know.

feelings:

_____

_____

_____

_____

seasonal focus:
buds unfold to early flowers.

Friday

morning focus
The angel of Air

meditation
Within the quiet of this morning
Stirs the constant movement
Of my breath.
The inbreath of my life-force
Draws the world to me.
And as the outbreath streams from me
I share my life with others.
So goes the process of my growth,
Inbreath, outbreath,
Giving, receiving,
And all is One.

evening focus
Our Heavenly Father

the blessing
Before you I stand, humble, yet assured,
A reflection of your own radiance
And perfection
As I grow.
I am my own gift to you,
My spiritual Father.
I am the promise of the new,
And I am ever mindful
Of the reason for my life.

feelings:

_____

_____

_____

_____

seasonal focus:
flowers announce the promise of fruit.

beltane
may 1

spiritual focus for this season

saturday
i will bring the spirit of authenticity to _____

sunday
i will bring the spirit of wholeness to _____

monday
i will bring the spirit of responsibility to _____

tuesday
i will bring the spirit of joy to _____

wednesday
i will bring the spirit of clarity to _____

thursday
i will bring the spirit of my divine nature to

_____

friday
i will bring the spirit of service to _____

feelings:

_____

_____

_____

_____

seasonal focus:
flowers announce the promise of fruit.

saturday

morning focus
Our Earthly Mother

meditation

I feel the presence
Of our Earthly Mother within me,
And that presence is illuminated
By the warm rays of the Father of us all.
All about me are the gifts
Of the Mother's ripening fruits,
And I know that in my own way
I am ripening too.

evening focus
The angel of Eternal Life

the blessing

Even as my fruits ripen,
As my gifts become manifest,
As I mature in openness and love,
I remember that
I have walked this path before,
And will again.
For the fruits of now
Contain the seeds of tomorrow,
And my seeds of bygone seasons
Have brought this day's joy to me.
My seeds, my fruits will come and go,
And I will carry on.

feelings:

_____

_____

_____

_____

seasonal focus:
flowers announce the promise of fruit.

sunday

morning focus
The angel of Earth

meditation
What is the source
From whence gushes the frenzied growth
All about me?
What overlighting presence
Guides the living things of earth
Toward the zenith of their life?
I, as one of these living things,
Marvel at the perfection
Of our unfolding.
Blessed am I to be a part
Of the Plan.

evening focus
The angel of Creative Work

the blessing
My heart tells me
That the time of compromise
Has passed.
Now, the work I do
Must nourish me
And heal the earth
And free our common spirit.

feelings:

___

___

___

___

seasonal focus:
flowers announce the promise of fruit.

monday

morning focus
The angel of Life

meditation
From the point from which all Life flows,
It flows to me.
My part is to accept this life consciously
As a manifestation of God on earth.
It is I
Who bring Light and Love
Into this existence.
No angelic being can do it for me.
Yes, heartily do I accept
This responsibility!
Yes, gladly do I accept
The God in me!

evening focus
The angel of Peace

the blessing
Throughout me there is movement;
There is growth
Streaming to the outer bounds
Of my potential,
And I feel full and overflowing.
Yet at my center,
At the very core of me,
There is a quiet place
From which my guidance comes.
Let me learn to seek this center often.

feelings:

_____

_____

_____

_____

seasonal focus:
flowers announce the promise of fruit.

tuesday

morning focus
The angel of Joy

meditation
From each moment
I draw life.
From each living being
I draw love.
From the earth and the sun
I draw nourishment.
From each I receive
And to each I joyfully give,
For the web that connects
Each to me
Weaves its tapestry
Throughout my being,
Uniting me with all.
Separateness
Is an illusion.

evening focus
The angel of Power

the blessing
As our sun
Daily shares more and more of its power with me,
I stand in awe of the power
That also lies within me.
I take upon myself the yoke of responsibility
For my power,
And direct that power
In the service of positive, liberating evolution
For myself and all beings.
So be it.

feelings:

_____

_____

_____

_____

seasonal focus:
flowers announce the promise of fruit.

wednesday

morning focus
The angel of the Sun

meditation
I enter into the season of the sun,
And the Sun within me responds in kind.
My heart tells me
To build my castles high
With love and clarity.
My soul tells me
To bring the Plan to earth.
My mind tells me
To bring perfection to my work.
There is much to do
And I am equal to the task.

evening focus
The angel of Love

the blessing
Many are the ways to share
The mystery that is me,
And the greatest of these is Love.
To love one another, truly,
Without expectation of gain,
Is to transform the world.
I am learning to move
Beyond possession and manipulation
And into the awareness of lovingness,
Where I need ask for naught
And simply share my love.

feelings:

___

___

___

___

seasonal focus:
flowers announce the promise of fruit.

thursday

morning focus
The angel of Water

meditation
A wave of the ocean glides over the sea
And crashes upon the shore.
My body dances over the meadow
And joyfully leaps in the air.
Is the wave not still one with the ocean?
Am I not one with All?
Can I separate myself from my Source
When that wellspring flows
Deep within me
And not on some distant mountain?

evening focus
The angel of Wisdom

the blessing
This is the season of searching outside me,
To discover the teachers who Know.
But deep within me I must remember
"When the Student is ready
The teacher appears."
When I ask the right questions
Answers always are there
For my teachers are everywhere.

feelings:

___

___

___

___

seasonal focus:
flowers announce the promise of fruit.

Friday

morning focus
The angel of Air

meditation
I can feel it, almost see it;
There is electricity in the air
Which urges life to live.
"Fully live," it calls to me,
"Fully know your Self,
Accept the challenge of your life,
Experience it all."

"I am the Word," God said,
"All this and more are you."
"I am the Word," I say to God,
"I accept your task for me."

evening focus
Our Heavenly Father

the blessing
It is I who asks
For your blessing, Father,
No longer in whimpered tones.
I have grown throughout the seasons
And stand now tall and sure.
I am sensing
Who I truly am,
And I stand to meet that test.
I am your Word within this life,
This lifetime
Know I this.

feelings:

___

___

___

___

seasonal focus:
the tree bends with ripened fruit.

summer solstice
june

spiritual focus for this season

saturday
i will bring the spirit of
love for all beings to

_____

sunday
i will bring the spirit of
my shining light to

_____

monday
i will bring the spirit of
connectedness to _____

tuesday
i will bring the spirit of
joyful sharing to _____

wednesday
i will bring the spirit of
fullness to _____

thursday
i will bring the spirit of
world peace to _____

friday
i will bring the spirit of
simplicity to _____

feelings:

___

___

___

___

seasonal focus:
the tree bends with ripened fruit.

saturday

morning focus
Our Earthly Mother

meditation
Lady, Mother of us all,
You are the source of all Love,
As the Father is the source of all Light.
You sustain me on my journey,
In my work,
In my service to my fellow beings.
May I be truly worthy
Of your Love.

evening focus
The angel of Eternal Life

the blessing
There is a vibration
That emanates from me
In whatever I do,
Mingling with,
Enhancing or detracting from
The universal vibration,
Depending upon the quality
Of my intent.
I commit myself
To a positive enhancement
Of the universal vibration
In each act and thought
That I create.

feelings:

_____

_____

_____

_____

seasonal focus:
the tree bends with ripened fruit.

sunday

morning focus
The angel of Earth

meditation
With the electric limits of my aura,
My personal energy field,
I tap the power
Of the earth in summer.
The earth current flows in me
And strengthens my body
For the work that only I can do
As a channel for the Light.
I feel it shine in me.

evening focus
The angel of Creative Work

the blessing
I am a builder,
A vehicle for creative perfection
To work itself upon the earth.
My task is clear and simple,
For I am the Plan unfolding,
And I am my work in progress.
The work goes well
And I give thanks.

feelings:

_____

_____

_____

_____

seasonal focus:
the tree bends with ripened fruit.

monday

morning focus
The angel of Life

meditation
My life is guided onward
Toward the Light.
All about me are the signs of growth,
The signs of new life
Bursting from containment.
I, too, feel this primal urge
To cast off limitation
And open my petals to the sun.
No longer must I wait.
I share my life with those I love.

evening focus
The angel of Peace

the blessing
Beauty surrounds me, beauty all around me.
Quiet beauty of the new flowers of springtime
Within me, the peaceful beauty of my being
Reflects the richness of my life.
And I am blessed.

feelings:

_____

_____

_____

_____

seasonal focus:
buds unfold to early flowers.

tuesday

morning focus
The angel of Joy

meditation
I am conscious of nature's outward thrust
In this season of the flowers,
And my heart is filled with joy.
The colors of my world,
The colors of my being,
The excitement of my life,
All these are the love of God
Shining upon my spirit.
There is no more that I need,
For I am complete.

evening focus
The angel of Power

the blessing
The joyful thrust of all of life,
Reaching for the sun,
Reminds me of the power that is mine
In the service of the Light.
May I remember always
That I am the server,
And that God is the Power.

feelings:

___

___

___

___

seasonal focus:
buds unfold to early flowers.

wednesday

morning focus
The angel of the Sun

meditation
The cells within my being
Respond to the call of
My spiritual father,
The sun.
As I grow,
As I expand to fill the outer limits
Of my potential,
I am nourished by the warmth
Of our ancient star
And I have all that
I could ever need
To guide me safely home.

evening focus
The angel of Love

the blessing
Who could not see,
Who could not feel,
The expression of divine Love
That fills the world this day?
As my buds softly open
Into rainbow flowers,
I return this Love
In every way I can.

feelings:

_____

_____

_____

_____

seasonal focus:
buds unfold to early flowers.

thursday

morning focus
The angel of Water

meditation
In my upward movement
Toward the perfect flower
That I truly am,
What feeds my inner being
But the waters of the earth,
Given by the Father to the Mother
And given back again?
Waters of the Spirit,
Waters of the earth,
Fill me fully with your life
And make me whole.

evening focus
The angel of Wisdom

the blessing
There is a knowing in this universe
That opens flowers in their time,
That gives me strength to grow.
The wisdom of this primal source
Is always mine to tap,
For I am one with all,
And all is mine to know.

feelings:

_____

_____

_____

_____

seasonal focus:
buds unfold to early flowers.

fRiday

morning focus
The angel of Air

meditation
Within the quiet of this morning
Stirs the constant movement
Of my breath.
The inbreath of my life-force
Draws the world to me.
And as the outbreath streams from me
I share my life with others.
So goes the process of my growth,
Inbreath, outbreath,
Giving, receiving,
And all is One.

evening focus
Our Heavenly Father

the Blessing
Before you I stand, humble, yet assured,
A reflection of your own radiance
And perfection
As I grow.
I am my own gift to you,
My spiritual Father.
I am the promise of the new,
And I am ever mindful
Of the reason for my life.

feelings:

___

___

___

___

seasonal focus:
flowers announce the promise of fruit.

beltane
may 1

spiritual focus for this season

saturday
i will bring the spirit of authenticity to _____

sunday
i will bring the spirit of wholeness to _____

monday
i will bring the spirit of responsibility to _____

tuesday
i will bring the spirit of joy to _____

wednesday
i will bring the spirit of clarity to _____

thursday
i will bring the spirit of my divine nature to

_____

friday
i will bring the spirit of service to _____

feelings:

_____

_____

_____

_____

seasonal focus:
flowers announce the promise of fruit.

saturday

morning focus
Our Earthly Mother

meditation
I feel the presence
Of our Earthly Mother within me,
And that presence is illuminated
By the warm rays of the Father of us all.
All about me are the gifts
Of the Mother's ripening fruits,
And I know that in my own way
I am ripening too.

evening focus
The angel of Eternal Life

the Blessing
Even as my fruits ripen,
As my gifts become manifest,
As I mature in openness and love,
I remember that
I have walked this path before,
And will again.
For the fruits of now
Contain the seeds of tomorrow,
And my seeds of bygone seasons
Have brought this day's joy to me.
My seeds, my fruits will come and go,
And I will carry on.

feelings:

_____

_____

_____

_____

seasonal focus:
flowers announce the promise of fruit.

sunday

morning focus
The angel of Earth

meditation
What is the source
From whence gushes the frenzied growth
All about me?
What overlighting presence
Guides the living things of earth
Toward the zenith of their life?
I, as one of these living things,
Marvel at the perfection
Of our unfolding.
Blessed am I to be a part
Of the Plan.

evening focus
The angel of Creative Work

the blessing
My heart tells me
That the time of compromise
Has passed.
Now, the work I do
Must nourish me
And heal the earth
And free our common spirit.

feelings:

___

___

___

___

seasonal focus:
flowers announce the promise of fruit.

monday

morning focus
The angel of Life

meditation

From the point from which all Life flows,
It flows to me.
My part is to accept this life consciously
As a manifestation of God on earth.
It is I
Who bring Light and Love
Into this existence.
No angelic being can do it for me.
Yes, heartily do I accept
This responsibility!
Yes, gladly do I accept
The God in me!

evening focus
The angel of Peace

the blessing

Throughout me there is movement;
There is growth
Streaming to the outer bounds
Of my potential,
And I feel full and overflowing.
Yet at my center,
At the very core of me,
There is a quiet place
From which my guidance comes.
Let me learn to seek this center often.

feelings:

_____

_____

_____

_____

seasonal focus:
flowers announce the promise of fruit.

tuesday

morning focus
The angel of Joy

meditation
From each moment
I draw life.
From each living being
I draw love.
From the earth and the sun
I draw nourishment.
From each I receive
And to each I joyfully give,
For the web that connects
Each to me
Weaves its tapestry
Throughout my being,
Uniting me with all.
Separateness
Is an illusion.

evening focus
The angel of Power

the blessing
As our sun
Daily shares more and more of its power with me,
I stand in awe of the power
That also lies within me.
I take upon myself the yoke of responsibility
For my power,
And direct that power
In the service of positive, liberating evolution
For myself and all beings.
So be it.

feelings:

_____

_____

_____

_____

seasonal focus:
flowers announce the promise of fruit.

wednesday

morning focus
The angel of the Sun

meditation
I enter into the season of the sun,
And the Sun within me responds in kind.
My heart tells me
To build my castles high
With love and clarity.
My soul tells me
To bring the Plan to earth.
My mind tells me
To bring perfection to my work.
There is much to do
And I am equal to the task.

evening focus
The angel of Love

the blessing
Many are the ways to share
The mystery that is me,
And the greatest of these is Love.
To love one another, truly,
Without expectation of gain,
Is to transform the world.
I am learning to move
Beyond possession and manipulation
And into the awareness of lovingness,
Where I need ask for naught
And simply share my love.

feelings:

___

___

___

___

seasonal focus:
flowers announce the promise of fruit.

thursday

morning focus
The angel of Water

meditation
A wave of the ocean glides over the sea
And crashes upon the shore.
My body dances over the meadow
And joyfully leaps in the air.
Is the wave not still one with the ocean?
Am I not one with All?
Can I separate myself from my Source
When that wellspring flows
Deep within me
And not on some distant mountain?

evening focus
The angel of Wisdom

the blessing
This is the season of searching outside me,
To discover the teachers who Know.
But deep within me I must remember
"When the Student is ready
The teacher appears."
When I ask the right questions
Answers always are there
For my teachers are everywhere.

feelings:

___

___

___

___

seasonal focus:
flowers announce the promise of fruit.

friday

morning focus
The angel of Air

meditation
I can feel it, almost see it;
There is electricity in the air
Which urges life to live.
"Fully live," it calls to me,
"Fully know your Self,
Accept the challenge of your life,
Experience it all."

"I am the Word," God said,
"All this and more are you."
"I am the Word," I say to God,
"I accept your task for me."

evening focus
Our Heavenly Father

the blessing
It is I who asks
For your blessing, Father,
No longer in whimpered tones.
I have grown throughout the seasons
And stand now tall and sure.
I am sensing
Who I truly am,
And I stand to meet that test.
I am your Word within this life,
This lifetime
Know I this.

Summer Solstice

feelings:

_____

_____

_____

_____

seasonal focus:
the tree bends with ripened fruit.

summer solstice
june

spiritual focus for this season

saturday
i will bring the spirit of love for all beings to

_____

sunday
i will bring the spirit of my shining light to

_____

monday
i will bring the spirit of connectedness to _____

tuesday
i will bring the spirit of joyful sharing to _____

wednesday
i will bring the spirit of fullness to _____

thursday
i will bring the spirit of world peace to _____

friday
i will bring the spirit of simplicity to _____

feelings:

_____

_____

_____

seasonal focus:
the tree bends with ripened fruit.

saturday

morning focus
Our Earthly Mother

meditation
Lady, Mother of us all,
You are the source of all Love,
As the Father is the source of all Light.
You sustain me on my journey,
In my work,
In my service to my fellow beings.
May I be truly worthy
Of your Love.

evening focus
The angel of Eternal Life

the blessing
There is a vibration
That emanates from me
In whatever I do,
Mingling with,
Enhancing or detracting from
The universal vibration,
Depending upon the quality
Of my intent.
I commit myself
To a positive enhancement
Of the universal vibration
In each act and thought
That I create.

feelings:

_____

_____

_____

_____

seasonal focus:
the tree bends with ripened fruit.

sunday

morning focus
The angel of Earth

meditation
With the electric limits of my aura,
My personal energy field,
I tap the power
Of the earth in summer.
The earth current flows in me
And strengthens my body
For the work that only I can do
As a channel for the Light.
I feel it shine in me.

evening focus
The angel of Creative Work

the blessing
I am a builder,
A vehicle for creative perfection
To work itself upon the earth.
My task is clear and simple,
For I am the Plan unfolding,
And I am my work in progress.
The work goes well
And I give thanks.

summer solstice

feelings:

_____

_____

_____

_____

seasonal focus:
the tree bends with ripened fruit.

monday

morning focus
The angel of Life

meditation
I have grown in wisdom
As this yearly wheel has turned.
I see
That freedom in my life
Is tied to that of all.
The springtime sense of Me Alone
Has mellowed and matured
Into the deeper knowing
That We are One.
Only when I respect the sacredness
Of all life shall I be truly free.

evening focus
The angel of Peace

the blessing
The core of peace
Lives not in thoughts,
Nor in the deeds I do.
It lives inside my heart,
In how I feel about me.
When I have learned to be at peace
Within myself,
Then shall I radiate
That peace to all.
Let me now go within
To calm the inner sea.

feelings:

___

___

___

___

seasonal focus:
the harvest is stored.

tuesday

morning focus
The angel of Joy

meditation
Softness fills my days
In this season of autumn light.
Gentle joy of life returning
To know its roots again.
Joyful completion
Of the outward surge of growth,
Preparing me for that to come
In the darkness before birth.
Who will I laugh with on this day,
Expecting nothing,
Sharing all?

evening focus
The angel of Power

the blessing
The shifting balance
From outward straightline movement
To inner spiral flow
Spins the wheel of my life inward,
And I must now transform
My restless yearnings
Into quiet contemplation
To aid me in the winter's inner journey
To the abundant core of me.

feelings:

_____

_____

_____

_____

seasonal focus:
the harvest is stored.

wednesday

morning focus
The angel of the Sun

meditation
This day will offer me another chance
To take within me
The lifeblood of the sun.
These lengthened rays of solar fire
Will be stored within my heart
If I but use this time to full advantage.
Let me study all the colors,
The shadings and the hues,
So that, when deep in winter's womb,
I may paint the portrait of the sun
With a memory
And share that scene with all.

evening focus
The angel of Love

the blessing
Out of the dance of summer
Comes the gathering of autumn
More gently now, more softly,
I gather with my friends
And touch the hands
That form the circle
And look into wiser eyes.
My love in comfort flows
From my life
To color all that is,
And blessed by other forms of God,
It flows quietly back to me.

feelings:

___

___

___

___

seasonal focus:
the harvest is stored.

thursday

morning focus
The angel of Water

meditation
There is a trickling of time in my life,
A cascading mountain stream of moments
That connect each spring and fall,
Each blossoming and harvesting.
What will be the colors of my flower
Come next Beltane time?
The answer lies in the ways
That I now prepare the soil
Of my inner garden,
And in how lovingly I water the seeds
From summer's fruit.

evening focus
The angel of Wisdom

the blessing
It has been said
That each of us has deep within
The knowledge of all things,
And when we are ready to remember
Then the knowledge is there
To be known.
This is the season of readying,
Of challenging old beliefs
That bind us to the past.
The millennium calls to me
To live the wisdom
Deep within me.

feelings:

_____

_____

_____

_____

seasonal focus:
the harvest is stored.

friday

morning focus
The angel of Air

meditation
There is a yearning in me now,
Which follows a season of outbreath.
It is the longing for the sweet inbreath
Of my spiritual nature.
And as my physical nature still urges me
To *do*,
Yet in my heart I know
My path leads me to *be*.
And I humbly honor the do-er in me
That makes my world revolve.
But now I prepare to take my inbreath
At the center
Of my Self.

evening focus
Our Heavenly Father

the blessing
You have brought me to the sun
And have filled me with its light.
You have strengthened my Will
And clarified my sight.
And now the eagle must fly
Back to the earth
And make ready to surrender
To the season of new birth.

feelings:

_____

_____

_____

_____

seasonal focus:
outer darkness calls for nourishment within.

samhain
november 1

spiritual focus for this season

saturday
i will bring the spirit of focused awareness to
_____

sunday
i will bring the spirit of aloneness to _____

monday
i will bring the spirit of new beginnings to ____

tuesday
i will bring the spirit of joyful music to _____

wednesday
i will bring the spirit of inner glow to_____

thursday
i will bring the spirit of purification to _____

friday
i will bring the spirit of clarity to _____

feelings:

_____

_____

_____

_____

seasonal focus:
outer darkness calls for nourishment within.

saturday

morning focus
Our Earthly Mother

meditation
The morning calls to me
To slow my pace and be,
To ease my crowded schedule
And perhaps just sit and stare.
To focus on a burning log,
On a raindrop on a leaf,
Or to find my own image
In a flickering candle flame.
The Mother's weather urges me
To let it go, let go.
A deep primal inner voice
Is whispering…within.

evening focus
The angel of Eternal Life

the blessing
I have seen the maple tree;
The leaves have left its limbs.
It stands bare and brittle now,
Its spirit gone within.
And in my mind I know
That deep within the earth
Its lifeblood pulses in its roots,
Rejuvenating strength.
How like that maple tree am I,
As I go within my core,
Experiencing outer death
And inner depth once more.

feelings:

_____

_____

_____

_____

seasonal focus:
outer darkness calls for nourishment within.

sunday

morning focus
The angel of Earth

meditation
The seed within the earth
Lies alone, awaiting.
It knows not loneliness,
But strength of purpose.
Throughout the year
I have known loneliness in crowds,
But aloneness is quite different.
I must pass through the gate
To the inner temple
Alone.

evening focus
The angel of Creative Work

the blessing
My inner wellspring bubbles over,
And the more I share
The more I have.
Help me to be of valued service,
Yet not attached to being a server.
For the tools of service
Are compassion and humility,
And these are born in a loving heart,
Which is open enough to take
As well as give.
From you I receive,
To you I give,
Together we share,
From this we live.

feelings:

___

___

___

___

seasonal focus:
outer darkness calls for nourishment within.

monday

morning focus
The angel of Life

meditation
As leaves fall to the earth
And surrender to the soil,
So I, too, move my attention
From my outward stance
To my inner Buddha nature.
The life in me flows back and forth
From exerting my will
To flowing with the Will of All.
And in this season of stillness,
My direction is clear
As I return unto my source.
The stillness calls to me.

evening focus
The angel of Peace

the blessing
The whispering of the candle flame
Invokes the peace within,
Reminding me of the quiet journey
That I seem to be on.
I have been given a peaceful heart
And a path to take me there.
May I joyfully take up this task
To reach the core of me,
And there to find all beings
Residing in my heart.

Samhain

feelings:

_____

_____

_____

_____

seasonal focus:
outer darkness calls for nourishment within.

tuesday

morning focus
The angel of Joy

meditation
This morning gives a song to me,
A lovely melody for me to play
Within my heart,
To give my spirit wings.
And I must close my eyes
To let the music come.
Unhurried, without force,
It yields its gift to me.
And just as gently I share this gift,
I hum this melody.
The air accepts,
The world is nourished,
And I become my song.
*(Allow some song or chant to come
to you in meditation and give it wings.)*

evening focus
The angel of Power

the blessing
Within my being lives
A silent power,
A firm, sound frame of wise
And compassionate strength.
How often do I deny this gift,
This blessing from my Source?
Perhaps as the outward power
Of the sun recedes in winter,
I will learn to own
The strength within.

Samhain

feelings:

_____

_____

_____

_____

seasonal focus:
outer darkness calls for nourishment within.

wednesday

morning focus
The angel of the Sun

meditation
You run from me,
You who have showered me
With light and warmth.
In summer's fullness
Was I nourished by your glow,
But now I must provide
This warmth myself.
The glow must be found
Within my heart,
The light within my spirit.
When next we meet in summer's glory,
I will wiser be.
Till then I take your light inwardly
With me.

evening focus
The angel of Love

the blessing
(On this evening, the Blessing takes the form of a love song, in the higher sense of Love.)

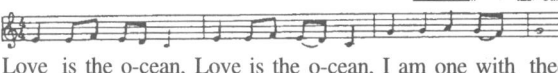

Love is the o-cean, Love is the o-cean, I am one with thee

Once a tiny lake, Now a mighty sea, Love, I am one with thee

Repeat, substituting the name of each person present for the word Love. If you sing the Blessing alone, use your name, and repeat the verse until you can allow it to be true for you.

Samhain

feelings:

_____

_____

_____

_____

seasonal focus:
outer darkness calls for nourishment within.

thursday

morning focus
The angel of Water

meditation
As I enter the sacred temple of inner knowing,
I purify my being
To prepare myself for the initiation
That I have longed to find.
I cleanse my mind and heart
As I strip away
Whatever stands between
My spirit and the source of All.
I make myself ready.
And I wait.
And it will come to me.

evening focus
The angel of Wisdom

the blessing
Ancient is the one in me
That the spirit of this season,
With its quiet murmur,
Calls.
Beyond, beneath the outer me,
My wise old seer
Looks out upon the dance
With compassion,
With a smile.
And the ancient one waits
For the young one
To knock upon the door.
And both of them
Are me.

feelings:

___

___

___

___

seasonal focus:
outer darkness calls for nourishment within.

friday

morning focus
The angel of Air

meditation
Each life upon this earthly plane
Knows beginning and knows ending.
Each turn of the yearly wheel as well
Brings birth and death.
Each breath I take reminds me, too,
That I must die each moment
So as to bring a blessed newness
To the next breath that I take.
For if each outbreath ends in death,
Each inbreath sees me born anew,
And present to that moment.

evening focus
Our Heavenly Father

the blessing
Throughout the flow of passing seasons,
You have shared your Light
With me.
No middle-person have I required
To walk the path with you.
For in my heart
You dwell forever,
Not in some mansion high,
And the blessings
That you give to me
Come from deep inside.

danaan parry
1939-1996

the essenes and me
by Danaan Parry

My *present* connection to the Essenes began with an "accidental" discovery in 1974. My friend Lila and I were at the Association for Research & Enlightenment (A.R.E.) in Virginia Beach, VA, which houses the library of research done on the life and "readings" of modern Christian mystic, Edgar Cayce. While pouring through the research on his ability to perform medical diagnoses on people while he was in a trance state, I began running into references to communities of white-robed spiritual seekers who lived in the deserts of the Holy Land around the time of Christ.

I remember my first encounter with these references to spiritual communities. It was in a reading/diagnosis for a middle-aged woman from Tennessee. In trance, Edgar Cayce said that her medical problem was only partially caused by dysfunction in her life today. He said that a good deal of it was residual from her life as an Essene in the community of Qumran, a hundred years before the birth of Jesus. He spoke of some conflict in that life that was still unresolved today, thereby leading to her imbalance. I found myself much more intrigued with Cayce's reference to the existence of this Essene community than to the medical diagnosis. I wondered who these people were and what they were doing in that barren land at that time? As I continued my studies of Cayce's readings, I came upon more references to these fascinating beings who walked out of major cities of the fertile crescent and gathered in communities in the most isolated parts of the desert. Cayce made vague reference to their common task, that of preparing the way for something very new and different. I was hooked.

I left the Cayce research and embarked upon a journey of

discovery. I was almost addicted to the need to find out who the Essenes were, and why I felt such a deep kinship to these obscure people who I had never heard of. It turned out that not many other people had heard of them either, although it was supposed that they were the ones who wrote the "Dead Sea Scrolls" which had been found in caves near the ruins of an ancient spiritual center outside of Jericho, Palestine near the old Qumran water hole. As I digested the meager writings available on the Essene from biblical scholars, and read the more popular writers like Edmund Bordeaux Szekely, I felt a bond of knowing growing between me and those dedicated visionaries of 2000 years ago. I felt their message of love for one another and of the earth come alive again, needing to be shared in today's troubled times. I packed my bags and went to Qumran.

A Carmelite monastery sits on a hill overlooking another ancient community of the Essenes, and in that monastery is a deep well. The well has been there long before the monastery was built during the Crusades. I know that it is the well of my brother and sister Essenes. I drank from this well, I slept on the stones of the ancient community and felt their message, as alive and as pertinent today as it was 2000 years ago. I hope that this book conveys that message in a form that they would find acceptable.

It took me a few years to integrate the nonlinear learning I experienced at Qumran, but when it was ready to come out, it came out like a freight train. One of the most important places for me on earth is a meadow high-up on the north face of Mount Shasta in Northern California. For years, I have been making an annual spiritual retreat to the mountain, camping out in that same meadow. It is my "power spot." In 1979 I again went to this meadow, but there would be no meditating for me there that year. In the middle of the first night I awoke, grabbed my journal and started writing. Four days later I was *still* writing. I had used every page of my journal, and every square inch of every scrap of paper and paper bag I had with me. When those four days and nights were over, I was exhausted, covered with sweat and higher than a kite. I had the essence of the *Essene Book of Days* down on paper. Every daily meditation, every evening blessing, the interplay of daily and seasonal energies, I had them all. It took another year to bring the book to publication, but that was just the mechanics.

As I look back on the years of integration of the Essene Way into my life, I see the effect they have had on me. My work in international conflict resolution looks very different than the simple lifestyle of the desert communities. But the seeds have been planted in me, and they bear fruit in the strangest ways. I am a preparer-of-the-way for something very new, as new and as needed as The Christ was needed 2000 years ago. And wherever I go, I meet my brothers and sisters who also quietly do their work of preparation. Perhaps you feel it too.

Each year I ask, "Should I change or update the Meditations?" And each year the message is given: "Leave them be; they were given." But most recently, I was told, "Prepare for the second cycle, the millennium." The seasonal flow of life-energy in this book has an important rhythm and consistency to it. It honors the part of us that is deeply rooted in the ebbs and flows of nature; the cycles of life, death and decay that lead to new birth. In our hectic lives, it is this connection to nature that gives us meaning, amidst the chaos that swirls around us. However . . . .

As we approached the year 2000, it seemed that we were being told to prepare for some important changes. The meditations now reflect these changes, so that we are ready for the challenge.

— Bainbridge Island, WA, 1996

about the author

On November 14, 1996, the world lost one of its finest citizens. Danaan Parry suffered a massive heart attack and passed away on Bainbridge Island, Washington. Despite this immense loss, Danaan's gifts as a global visionary will continue to bless the human family for generations to come.

Danaan John Raymond Parry, born in Orange, New Jersey, spent his childhood on the Jersey shore and was a helicopter pilot for the US Coast Guard. After working for the US Atomic Energy Commission as a research physicist, he became a clinical psychologist and taught at the Graduate Theological Union in Berkeley, California.

Eventually, his interest in expanding the human consciousness led to a meeting with Mother Teresa in Bombay. There he realized the need to bring spirituality down off the mountain. As a co-founder of the Earthstewards Network, he decided to dedicate his life to conflict resolution work around the world.

Through his teaching of the *Warriors of the Heart* and *Essential Peacemaking* workshops offered by the Earthstewards Network as well as his writings on the Essenes, thousands of people have been inspired to tap their own natural ability and spiritual resources to lead more effective lives and to help others.

Danaan's last gift to the world was the creation of PeaceTrees Vietnam. He started this program with his wife, Jerilyn Brusseau, and the help of many dedicated volunteers. Under this program, hundreds of landmines have been removed from the Quang Tri Province in Vietnam. The land is then revitalized through tree planting by international citizens, including many US veterans of the war, working with Vietnamese citizens.

PeaceTrees Vietnam and the other works of the Earthstewards Network symbolize Danaan's commitment to practical mysticism: inspiring individuals to take action in circumstances which seem hopeless and out of reach.

the earthstewards network & our publications

· earthsteward network membership ·

When you become an Earthsteward, you become a part of an exciting network of people who support one another as they co-create a more peaceful, caring world. Members are invited to participate in trainings, trips and special projects, including the annual network-wide Earthstewards Gatherings. Members receive the Earthstewards Network Newsletter and regular informational updates concerning projects and programs. For more information on the Network, please see our web page at: www.earthstewards.org. One year membership, $40.00 (includes shipping)

· books & cassettes ·

Essene Book of Days is a daily journal, calendar and guide for those on a path of personal and spiritual growth. Each page contains special reminders of astrological and seasonal changes for that day. Trade paperback. 416 pp. *Danaan Parry* ($15.95)

Essene Book of Meditations & Blessings serves as gentle reminder to seasonal changes. Revised second edition contains nearly 20 more pages and more space to write your thoughts and feelings. 4" by 6"; 144 pp. *Danaan Parry* ($6.95)

Warriors of the Heart is a handbook for bringing healing, passion and meaning to your life and relationships. Based on Danaan Parry's conflict resolution work around the world. 5th edition (1997), trade paperback, 224 pp. *Danaan Parry* ($12.95)
Live audio workshop also available on cassette ($9.95)

earthstewards network order form

If your local bookstore doesn't carry our titles, please mail this order form or call the 1-800 phone number listed below.

Ship to (Name & Address):

TITLE	Price	Qty	Total
Earthstewards 1 yr membership	$40.00		
Essene Bk of Days 20____*	$15.95		
Essene Bk Meditations/Blessings	$6.95		
Warriors of the Heart	$12.95		
Warriors (cassette)	$9.95		

*Please specify year for Book of Days. Next year available by August: i.e. 2002 Book available by 08/01
**WA state residents only, add 8.2% sales tax.

Shipping	
Tax**	
Total	

Shipping and Handling *per U.S. location*. Others sent international surface. **Internat'l air add $10**.

Merchandise Total	U.S.	Others Add
up to $10.00	3.50	5.50
$10.01-$20.00	4.50	6.50
$20.01-$30.00	5.00	11.50
$30.01-$60.00	6.00	13.00
over $60.00	7.00	15.00

☐ VISA ☐ M/C
☐ Check or money order enclosed

CC#

Exp Date

Signature Required

Mail to:
Earthstewards Network Publications
PO Box 10697 Bainbridge Island WA 98110

206-322-6442 or 800-561-2909